NON-FICTION

HURRICANES AND FLOODS

ANNE SCHRAFF

Artesian **Press**

P.O. Box 355, Buena Park, CA 90621

Non Fiction
Natural Disaster Series

Blizzards	1-58659-200-9
Audio Cassette	1-58659-116-9
Audio CD	1-58659-350-1
Earthquakes	1-58659-201-7
Audio Cassette	1-58659-117-7
Audio CD	1-58659-351-X
Hurricanes and Floods	**1-58659-202-5**
Audio Cassette	**1-58659-118-5**
Audio CD	**1-58659-352-8**
Tornadoes	1-58659-203-3
Audio Cassette	1-58659-119-3
Audio CD	1-58659-353-6
Wildfires	1-58659-204-1
Audio Cassette	1-58659-120-7
Audio CD	1-58659-354-4

Cover image courtesy MODIS Rapid Response Project at NASA/GSFC
Project Editor: Molly Mraz
Illustrator: Fujiko
Graphic Design: Tony Amaro
©2004 Artesian Press

 **Artesian Press**   ISBN 1-58659-202-5

CONTENTS

Chapter 1

Something was wrong in Texas the summer of 1900. The heat wave was worse than anything the old-timers had ever seen. Worse yet were the crickets. There were crickets everywhere--wall-to-wall crickets--in Waco, Texas, and no one could figure it out.

It was boiling hot in Galveston, Texas, in September. Then it started to rain. At first, the rain was a welcome relief from the heat. But then it kept coming down, heavier and heavier. By Friday, September 7, anyone could see that a big storm was underway.

A young man named Isaac Cline

was head of the Texas Weather Bureau, and he said not to worry. There would be some wind and rain, but nothing the city could not handle. Although the ocean swells in the Gulf of Mexico looked dark and dangerous, Cline said it would be a mild storm.

But down in Cuba, the weather experts were saying something very different. They warned that a huge, dangerous storm was heading for the United States. They said the Gulf Coast should be prepared.

The trouble was, no one paid much attention to what the Cubans were saying. The United States had just won the Spanish-American War and freed Cuba from Spain. The Americans did not believe that the Cuban weathermen knew more than the Americans. So they ignored the Cuban warnings.

Then the toads started appearing on the Galveston beaches. No one could remember seeing so many toads hopping on the sand. Something had driven them from their island homes, and now they swarmed onto the beaches. Some people became nervous because of the heat, the crickets, and now the toads. Something was wrong.

Galveston was a big, booming city in 1900. It was the second-richest city in the United States. (The richest was Newport, Rhode Island.) Galveston

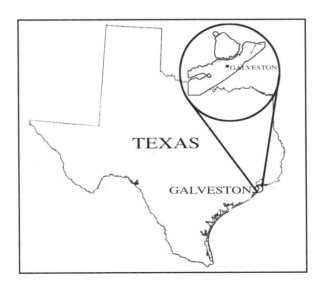

was called the "New York of the Gulf." About 38,000 people lived there in fine homes on wide streets. Galveston was beautiful. There were rosebushes, graceful palm trees, and white, pink, and red flowers called oleanders. It was both a seaside resort and a thriving port. It seemed impossible that anything really bad could happen in such a lovely place.

On Friday morning, September 7, the rainfall was so heavy that Mr. Cline had to calm the people of the city down. On September 8, many people got up early to go down to the beaches and watch the unusually high waves.

They were the biggest waves anybody could remember. It was exciting to see them breaking on the beach. People screamed in delight as they outran the ever-growing waves. Water splashed into the streets of Galveston, and children made little boats from sticks and floated them in front of their homes. People collected driftwood that was washed up onto their front lawns. Some streets turned into shallow canals, and it was fun to watch.

Suddenly, a flimsy little beach house built on the sand crumbled and blew apart. The waves smashed it into firewood. The people watching on the beach were startled, but not frightened. The beach house was too close to the water. True, it had stood for a long time, but these waves were very big.

Slowly, the water flowing into the streets of the city got too deep. The playing children abandoned their boats and ran to their homes, a little afraid now. At 10 A.M., the Washington Weather Bureau sent a telegram with some very bad news to Isaac Cline. They said that a serious storm—possibly deadly—was bearing down on Galveston. Isaac Cline said it was absurd to think that serious damage could be done to the city.

By noon, the winds were blowing at 30 miles per hour. Each hour after that, the wind speed grew in power. Rain was pelting Galveston with great fury now. The Gulf of Mexico was flowing into the streets closest to the beach. The water was already 3 to 4 feet deep in some places. A few beach homes, battered by wind and waves, started to fall apart. The disaster had begun.

Chapter 2

Galveston is situated on a long, narrow island at the southern end of Galveston Bay. On one side of the island is the bay and on the other is the Gulf of Mexico. Connecting the island to mainland Texas was a wagon bridge and a railroad trestle, which supported the bridge. The water was rising so fast by midday, September 8, that the bridge and the trestle had vanished beneath floodwaters. The routes of escape for the people of Galveston were gone, and 38,000 people were trapped on an island with a powerful hurricane bearing down on them.

A hurricane is a large storm with

winds greater than 74 miles per hour, bringing torrential rain or a violent stream of water. When a hurricane comes ashore, it brings tons of water in a large wave. The water crashes into land, doing terrible damage.

These huge storms do not sneak up on people. Weather experts see them coming. The hurricane threatening Galveston was first spotted way back on August 27, 1900. By September 4, as it passed over Cuba, there were warnings. By September 5, as wind and rain lashed the Florida Keys, the storm was gathering speed like a locomotive. But all this information was ignored until it was too late.

At 2:30 P.M., even Isaac Cline accepted the fact that Galveston was in trouble. He telegraphed Washington, D.C., with this grim message: "Gulf rising rapidly, half the city now under water." He predicted a great loss of life. It was the last message sent from

Galveston before the full impact of the terrifying storm hit.

Isaac Cline's wife, Cora May, was pregnant with the family's fourth child. The other three children were twelve-year-old Allie May, eleven-year-old Rosemary, and six-year-old Esther.

The family lived in a very sturdy home three blocks from the Gulf of Mexico. Like many Galveston homes, the Clines' house was built on stilts to keep it above the high water that often came during rainstorms. Because the neighbors believed that the house was the strongest in the neighborhood, many of them joined the Clines as the storm got worse.

After 2:30 P.M., Cline returned home to find his family, including his brother, Joseph, and fifty neighbors taking refuge there. Joseph was very alarmed, and he wanted everyone to evacuate the house immediately.

Isaac Cline believed it was safer to remain, so they did.

At 3:15, people saw what appeared to be a 50-foot wall of gray water rising from the Gulf and heading for Galveston. Many ran to higher ground, but the Cline family remained in the house.

At 5:30 P.M., on the first floor of the Cline house, the water was waist-deep. When Isaac Cline opened the front door, he stared out at a bleak world. It was dusk, making the storm appear even more frightening. Everything looked like a wide sea.

Houses all around the Cline home had already collapsed. Because of the tidal surge, the water rose 4 feet in just 4 seconds, and Cline realized it was time to go.

As the Clines prepared to escape, the Gulf of Mexico was now 10 feet deep in the street. It rose to 15 feet before another hour had passed. At

7:00 P.M., it was totally dark, and winds were rushing through the city at 120 miles per hour.

Debris from the ruins of neighboring houses battered the Cline house. A railroad trestle, one-quarter of a mile long, was pounding the house. At 7:30, as the Clines were leaving, the wind shifted, attacking the house from the other side. The Cline house began to tilt like a sinking ship. The fifty screaming people tumbled across the floor like toys scattered by a toddler. The house rocked and then tumbled sideways.

Joseph Cline grabbed the hands of Allie May and Rosemary, and the three of them jumped through a second-floor window. Once outside in the wild, debris-filled sea, they swam to the rooftop of another house, which was floating nearby. They climbed onto the roof and huddled there together.

Isaac Cline, his wife, and youngest daughter, Esther, tried to escape the same way, but when the house rolled over, they were sucked underneath. They plunged into the swirling darkness.

Chapter 3

Knocked unconscious by some debris, Isaac Cline awoke to find himself floating in the water. He saw Esther frantically clinging to a piece of a house. He did not see his wife. He swam to Esther and grabbed her hand. They managed to reach the roof where Joseph and the other children were.

When the roof began to totter and overturn, the five of them jumped onto other debris. The sea was filled with sharp, jagged boards with nails sticking out of them. Under attack by these dangerous objects, the Clines held up pieces of wood to defend themselves. Some of the other survivors in the large, violent whirlpool were slashed and killed by pieces of destroyed houses and stores.

All over Galveston, thousands of people fought similar battles for their lives. St. Mary's Orphanage had been built near the water because people believed this location was safer from the yellow-fever epidemics that raged inland. The Sisters of Charity, a Roman Catholic order of nuns, sheltered ninety-three orphans at the institution.

Both buildings were wooden, but the girls' dormitory was stronger than the boys'. So, as the storm worsened, the nuns gathered the boys from their rooms and brought them into the girls' building. Everyone watched from the window as the crashing sea carried the boys' dormitory away.

As the rain and wind grew more powerful, the nuns led the children to the second floor. To calm the orphans, the nuns led them in singing the old French sailors' song "Queen of the Waves."

The nuns were afraid that the children might be swept away. They tied clothesline around the waist of each child and then around their own waists. The ten nuns and ninety-three orphans huddled together and sang as the storm raged.

Suddenly, an enormous surge of water lifted the whole building off its foundation, hurling it down with a deafening crash. Between 7:00 and 8:00 P.M., the women and children were all swept underneath the falling dormitory.

Later, the bodies of all ten nuns and ninety of the children were found. One nun had nine small children still tied to her. Another held a child in each arm. They died clinging to one another.

Only three orphans, all boys,

survived. They had somehow been swept into the open sea, where they grabbed passing trees, clinging to them, until the waters went down.

Across the city, a pregnant woman clung to the roof of her house, which was underwater. A surging wave tore her from the roof and hurled her into the wild water. She grabbed a trunk and held on as it bobbed in the spinning waters. Finally, the trunk was smashed against the wall of a convent that was still standing. The nuns saw the pregnant woman floundering in the sea, and they dragged her inside the convent. A few hours later, she gave birth to a healthy baby boy.

Many of the women floating in the floodwaters got their long hair caught in the branches of uprooted trees. As they hung there, they were often cut by the sharp debris that floated by. One man was beheaded by a piece of slate torn from a roof. It came at him with such force that his head was instantly severed.

Telegraph poles floated like straws in the water, and huge chunks of bricks were hurled at the buildings that still stood. Galveston was coming apart, piece by piece.

Slate shingles had been turned into whirling blades, injuring and killing people. Streetcar tracks slashed at people like knives. People clung desperately to one another as the wind speeds increased to 135 miles per hour. The Gulf of Mexico merged with the Bay of Galveston, causing the city to disappear beneath the waters.

At around 10:30 P.M., the winds at last began to die down. Isaac Cline, his brother, and his daughters had survived. Cora May Cline's battered body was discovered weeks later under their shattered home.

Chapter 4

Even the dead were not spared in the Galveston flood and hurricane. Throughout the city, bodies were washed out of their graves in the cemeteries.

As dawn broke on Galveston on September 9, a scene of unbelievable horror appeared. The once-beautiful city had become a great mound of wreckage. The dead lay everywhere. Most of them were naked. The jagged debris had ripped off their clothing. The dazed survivors were mostly naked, too. People were wrapped in whatever rags they could find.

Entire families in Galveston were wiped out. Every family lost at least

This photograph shows the damage the hurricane and flood caused to Galveston.

one member. Galveston Bay was jammed with the dead bodies of men, women, children, cows, horses, chickens, and dogs. Two-thirds of the city was destroyed.

At least 6,000 people––perhaps as many as 10,000––died. Thousands more were injured. Half of all the houses in Galveston were completely gone. Not a single building escaped damage. The city lay in ruins.

As the storm faded, the smothering heat returned. The people knew that it was very important to get rid of all the dead bodies immediately to prevent deadly diseases from breaking out. The odor from the dead bodies was already so strong that it made sailors on ships windward of Galveston sick.

First, they tried burial at sea. Bodies were loaded onto barges, taken out to sea, and shoved overboard. But the tide brought them back. They had to find another way.

Some of the dead were buried where they fell. The ten nuns and ninety orphans were buried in a mass grave where the orphanage once stood.

Many bodies were burned. There were huge funeral bonfires, and dark, sickening smoke hung in the air over Galveston for days.

There was no time for funerals. The work was urgent. Almost one in every six people died. Many more were injured. Thousands were homeless. The terrible work of burning and burying the dead became the job of every able-bodied man in Galveston.

Those who tried to refuse the duty were forced to work at the point of a bayonet. The men drank whiskey while they worked. It was the only way they could finish the awful task.

Isaac Cline, whose unwillingness to see the oncoming disaster made it worse, took the ring off his dead wife's finger. He had the ring recast to fit his own finger. He wore it from then on. Though he was just thirty-eight years old when his wife died, Cline never remarried. He mourned his wife and his dead unborn child for the rest of his life.

The Galveston hurricane and flood was the deadliest natural disaster in American history. Never before had so many Americans died in a single disaster.

When the authorities in Galveston noticed that the wreckage from the storm had created a kind of sea wall in the middle of the city, protecting the land behind it, they got an idea. A 17-foot sea wall was built in Galveston so that the horror of 1900 could never happen again. In fact, a very similar hurricane hit the city, just fifteen years later, and only eight people died. A cement causeway was also built so that Galveston would never again be cut off from the world.

Scientists group all violent wind and rainstorms together as tropical cyclones. Those in the Indian Ocean and around Australia are called cyclones. In the Pacific, they are called typhoons. Those that come from the Atlantic Ocean, the Caribbean sea, or the Gulf of Mexico are called hurricanes.

The word *hurricane* comes from Huracan, the Caribbean god of stormy weather.   The target of tropical cyclones is usually a tropical country. The toll in human life can be incredible, especially when a country like Bangladesh is struck.

Chapter 5

Bangladesh is located on the northeastern corner of the Indian continent. The 75 million people who live there faced 150 mile-per-hour winds and a 20-foot tidal wave in April 1991. Called Cyclone 2B, it roared out of the Bay of Bengal. It reduced thousands of homes to rubble and killed 140,000 people. Earlier, in 1970, another cyclone in Bangladesh took 300,000 lives. This was the greatest loss of life in the twentieth century from any natural disaster except for floods in China.

Florida has been the site of many dangerous hurricanes, but none worse than the Okeechobee hurricane and flood in 1928. On September 16 of that year, a hurricane roared across Palm Beach County in Florida. The fierce winds reached into Lake Okeechobee and literally sucked tons of water up into the sky, only to send the water crashing back down. The countryside around the lake was drowned in water and mud. One survivor of the hurricane said it was like seeing the moon crash down on the earth.

Most of the dead were migrant workers from the Caribbean and poor farmers, so the death toll was underestimated for a long time. Recently, it was raised from the inaccurate figure of 700 to at least 2,500, but there were probably many more.

The Saffir-Simpson scale is used to measure the power of hurricanes. It goes from category 1, where damage is minor, to category 5, where it is catastrophic.

On Labor Day, 1935, a category 5 hurricane struck the Florida Keys, killing six hundred people. In 1969, another category 5 called Hurricane Camille took 256 lives and caused more than $1 billion in property damage.

In spite of the timely warnings before Hurricane Camille struck, there was another kind of tragedy during the storm. Throughout the regions where hurricanes occur, there is the strange, dangerous tradition of "hurricane parties." Foolhardy people ignore the warnings to evacuate low-lying areas. Instead, they stay in dangerous locations and celebrate the oncoming storm. Such an event happened in the Richelieu Apartments of Pass Christian, Mississippi, as Hurricane Camille bore down on the coast.

Twelve residents of the apartments

began partying on the third floor as the weather bureau warned of 200 mile-per-hour winds coming their way. They stocked up on party food and beverages and prepared to watch the high waves from their windows.

The merrymakers believed Camille would strike east of their location, and the worst they would have to deal with would be high waves and some wind. As the party got underway, another dozen residents of the apartments decided to join the festivities. They never made it to the third floor.

Hurricane Camille hit Pass Christian directly. The surf rose 19 feet above the high-tide line. A giant wave came roaring in from the sea. It struck the apartments and smashed the large picture windows.

Within five minutes, water was pouring into the second-story windows, drowning the people there.

The whole building collapsed into the whirling sea. Of the twenty-four people who stayed to watch the storm, twenty-three died. One woman was carried 5 miles by the water and thrown into a treetop. She was the only survivor.

Chapter 6

Hurricanes are named from a list of twenty-one common male and female names. A different list is used each year for six years, then the list is repeated. Once a storm has caused severe damage, the name is retired forever. This happened to the name *Andrew* in August 1992.

Hurricane Andrew was the most expensive natural disaster ever to hit the United States. Damages exceeded $30 billion, but advance warnings kept the death toll remarkably low.

Hurricanes erupt out of tropical storms. Scientists at the National Hurricane Center track a growing storm using weather satellites. Once it becomes a full-blown hurricane, Air Force planes head for the eye of the storm. (The eye is the calm center of a hurricane.) The crewmembers plot the location and direction the storm may take, then issue a hurricane watch.

When there is a likelihood of a hurricane striking within twenty-four hours, a hurricane warning is given. People board up their homes and businesses and leave the area. That is what happened when Hurricane Andrew hit southern Florida. Its winds were 155 miles per hour, making it one of only three category 5 hurricanes ever to hit the United States.

One survivor of the hurricane who lived in Homestead, Florida, boarded up all the windows before the winds came. The hurricane ripped the boards off the windows and sprayed the rooms with broken glass. At one point, the man and his son were holding the front door against the wind. It had a dead-bolt lock. The bottom and top of the door were pushed in by the wind, but the door held. The entire house began to shake. Pictures fell from the walls, and the walls themselves bent with the force of the wind.

Hurricane Andrew's winds were so strong, they drove plywood and wood boards through the trunks of palm trees. The force of the wind was so intense that it ripped an 80-foot steel beam that weighed several tons from a building and hurled it a block away. Miles of houses and stores were leveled in the hurricane. In spite of the awesome devastation, which required thousands of people to live in temporary housing for several years, only twenty-six people died. That shows how important warning systems and evacuations are.

National Oceanic and Atmospheric Administration/ Historic NWS Collection.

Hurricane Andrew's winds were so strong that they drove a piece of plywood through the trunk of this royal palm tree.

People can also take steps to prevent other disasters, such as floods. The Hwang He is the major river of northern China. *Hwang* means "yellow," so it is often called the Yellow River. The Hwang He begins high in Tibet and flows more than 2,900 miles through China. Heavy seasonal rains have often flooded the low, flat plain. This is why the Hwang He is called "China's sorrow."

In August 1931, a terrible flood in China claimed 3,700,000 lives. Since then, dikes, or walls, were built to keep the Hwang He from flooding the land, so there has been less destruction in recent years.

Sometimes a great rush of deadly water does not come as the result of a hurricane or a flooded river. Sometimes unexpected heavy rains are enough to create a disaster.

At the foot of the Sierra Madre Mountains is Los Angeles. The city usually gets about 11 inches of rain during the year, which is not enough. However, in late February 1938, it began to rain and wouldn't quit. For five days, very heavy rain, called torrential rain, came down from gray skies. The rain turned small mountain streams into rushing rivers that flowed into the suburbs near the mountains. Eleven inches of rain, the normal season total, fell in just five days. On March 3, Los Angeles was cut off from the world with no telephone or telegraph lines.

Thousands of people ran from their flooding homes and took refuge in schools, theaters, and other public buildings. Motorists, suddenly marooned by raging floodwaters at intersections, climbed to the roofs of their cars and shouted for help. Some were rescued and some were washed away. Walls of water spilled from higher elevations and created mounds of silt, or sand and soil, below. Bridges and homes were severely damaged or smashed by the flood.

When the sun finally came out on March 4, Los Angeles looked like a muddy disaster area. At least seventy people were dead, including eighteen children. Many more were feared buried.

Chapter 7

Sometimes, heavy rainfall isn't needed to create a torrent of deadly water. On the night of March 12, 1928, the lights of Los Angeles blinked ominously.

It was 11:57 P.M., and the windows of Los Angeles rattled strangely. The lights went out for a second or two. Nobody expected what was about to happen.

In the San Francisquito Canyon, above Power Plant No. 2, a dam held 12 billion gallons of water. A muffled roar filled the night as hundreds in the path of destruction slept peacefully.

As the dam broke, an employee of

the San Francisquito Dam saw a 120-foot wave beginning its deadly journey into the valley. He climbed to the roof of a building. Nearby, 150 workers were asleep in tents. Within minutes, the water had swept them away, drowning them all.

The powerful tide of water made its way down the narrow Santa Clara Valley all the way to Santa Paula, 50 miles away. Ahead were prosperous farms, houses, and bridges. In a short time, it would all be gone, almost without a trace.

On Highway 126 in the Santa Clara Valley, about fifty automobiles were moving through the darkness. They carried about 125 men, women, and children. The floodwaters overcame them all. The cars were carried along with the water as it rushed toward the ocean. Large pieces of the broken dam were also carried downstream in the growing tide of debris.

There were four hundred homes in San Francisquito canyon between the dam and the little town of Piru. They had no warning. They had no chance. The houses were so completely wiped out that not even a single piece of wood remained standing. It was as though nothing had ever been built there. Telephone poles, fences, bridges, and railroad tracks were ripped from the earth by the force of the water.

Some of the cars--with people still inside--were found twenty miles away from where they had been struck by the giant wave of floodwater. Many of the cars and people who were swept away were never found.

The torrent moved across the land in a 2-mile-wide path. The remains of houses, stores, and people finally were washed into the Pacific Ocean.

When it was over, the death toll was estimated at 450.

There had been a defect in the dam, the experts said. The builder of the dam took full responsibility. For weeks after the disaster, bodies tightly packed in mud were found. Years later, human remains washed up on the beaches of the Pacific Ocean. The dam was never rebuilt.

But the catastrophe that stands as the greatest and most tragic involving a dam happened many years earlier. Both human foolishness and heavy rain combined to cause a deadly event.

Torrential rain pounded the mountains of western Pennsylvania in the spring of 1889. At 4:07 P.M. on May 31, the people of Johnstown heard a low rumble. It grew in intensity until it was a deafening roar. The people were instantly afraid, because they knew just what was happening. They had feared this event for a long time. The dam was giving way.

Johnstown was a steel company town with a population of 30,000. It was built on a flood plain at the fork of the Little Conemaugh and Stony Creek rivers. Fourteen miles up the Little Conemaugh, there was a 3-mile-long lake on a mountain 450 feet above Johnstown. That was where the dam had been built.

The South Fork Dam, as it was called, had been in need of repair. It should have been gradually drained and abandoned. But a group of rich men had other plans for the dam, plans that would result in the destruction of Johnstown.

Chapter 8

The Johnstown flood had been called the worst natural disaster of the nineteenth century, but some refused to call it a natural disaster at all. They blamed sixty-one men from Pittsburgh who rebuilt the defective South Fork Dam into a playground for their own use, ignoring safety precautions. The men made a 70-foot lake in the middle of what became their private club.

The job of repairing the old dam went to a railroad contractor, not an engineer. An engineer would have understood the danger in having a weak dam, which was strained to the breaking point when it rained, and was perched over the city.

The contractor shored up the dam with rocks, tree stumps, and mud. The owners' cottages were built away from the dam, and the South Fork Fishing and Hunting Club was in business.

Minutes before the dam broke, some of the club's employees tried to warn the people below that they had heard cracking sounds. No one took the warnings seriously. One man rode a big horse through town and yelled, "Run to the hills, the reservoir is breaking!" The people thought he was a madman.

The roar of the collapsing dam mingled with the frantic wail of a train whistle. The engineer of a train coming down into the valley saw the danger and tried to alert the people to what was coming. The train was racing ahead of the wall of water.

One family, consisting of six-year-old Elsie, four-year-old Eva, three-year-old Fanny, and their parents, heard the train whistle and immediately understood the warning.

Mr. Schaffer, the father, grabbed Elsie and Eva while his wife got Fanny. The Schaffers raced up the nearby hill, escaping the flood by seconds. No sooner had they reached the top of the hill than their house exploded under the pressure of the flood.

A 40-foot wall of water was bearing down on Johnstown at the speed of 40 miles per hour. It destroyed everything in its path. Thousands of people scrambled for higher ground, but many were overtaken by the torrent of muddy water and drowned. Debris from uprooted trees and shattered buildings collided with the people caught in the water, injuring some and killing others.

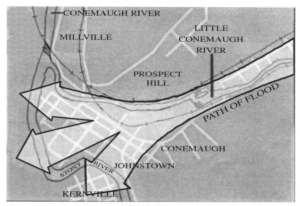

Map of the flood's path through Johnstown.

The wild water carried away steel mills, houses, livestock, and people. It ravaged Johnstown for ten long minutes. The floodwaters scooped up soil down to the bare rock. Houses and other wooden buildings were reduced to splinters.

Crying, screaming people clung to whatever debris they could find in an effort to ride the floodwaters. As darkness fell, thousands of people were huddled in the attics of houses that had survived but were damaged. Many more had been swept downstream, and now they clung to pieces of lumber, using them like rafts.

One woman managed to get herself and her six children aboard a detached roof that was floating in the water. But the roof tilted, and one by one the children slipped off into the water. They were swept out of sight. When the woman was rescued, she cried that she had nothing more to live for.

Although the floodwaters that swept through and destroyed most of the town were now going down, the worst was yet to come for some of the survivors.

Chapter 9

The floodwaters were now jammed with every kind of debris imaginable, from tangled, smashed wagons to lumber from destroyed buildings. Thirty city blocks had been leveled, and the remains formed a 30-foot-high mountain of wreckage. The mountain of debris, with many survivors riding it, reached the old Stone Bridge and was stopped by the arches of the bridge. About eighty people were trapped in the rubble when the entire mass caught fire.

The fire, ignited by hot embers from coal stoves ripped from houses, flamed into an inferno. People who had survived the flood were now surrounded by the fire. Those who did not burn tumbled into the water to drown. All eighty of the people trapped in the debris perished.

The Johnstown flood killed more than 2,200 people. There were 565 children who lost one or both parents in the disaster.

In the days after the tragedy, the refugees huddled in tents. Twenty thousand people were homeless. There was a great danger of typhoid fever breaking out because unburied bodies filled the swampy land. There were no sewage facilities. The entire area was foul with the smell of dead people and animals.

The flood had cut off all communication, and for a while, Johnstown was isolated in its misery. But when communication was restored, hundreds of volunteers poured in, including doctors and ministers. Martial law was established to stop some small groups of looters. When looting did occur, angry survivors of the flood promptly shot the looters.

Rescuers who came to Johnstown dug for bodies deeply buried in the mud. At one point, they were finding bodies at the rate of five a minute. Carloads of disinfectants were sent into Johnstown to try to prevent disease from breaking out.

Many of the bodies found were never identified because entire families died, and there was no one left to identify them. In many cases, every person on a street died, and not even a neighbor was left to identify the dead.

The cleanup of Johnstown took several years. Some missing bodies were not found until years after the flood. It took Johnstown five long years to get back to normal.

Everyone in Johnstown knew

Johnstown was completely devastated by the flood.

where to place the blame for the disaster. There was no question that the dam was poorly built—a disaster waiting to happen. The heavy rainfall of that spring was all that was needed to break the dam wide open.

Many lawsuits were filed against the men who built the shoddy dam, but all of them failed. The people who suffered the loss of loved ones and property never saw a penny in compensation.

Some countries have fought a long-standing battle against water surging across their land. The western region of the Netherlands was once a vast swamp. Ancient people there built their homes on mounds of earth above the water.

With the use of windmills and other devices, the Netherlands had reclaimed much land. But in 1953, huge 100-mile-per-hour waves smashed into the land, killing almost 2,000 people. Newer dikes have been built to prevent another such disaster.

In Italy, where some major cities were built at sea level, floods are a threat. In the fall of 1966, Florence, Italy, was the victim of heavy rains. The rains fell daily, leading eventually to a major disaster. After steady rainfall in October, the skies finally seemed to be clearing. On November 3, the skies darkened and the rainfall returned, pounding the city with amazing intensity.

Chapter 10

The torrential rains battered Florence. In just two days, an incredible 19 inches of rain fell. Florence had suffered floods before because it was built on low-lying land. Adding to the problem, many of the trees in the forests on nearby mountains had been cut down, so they no longer protected the land from erosion. The steep, rocky ravines above the city quickly turned into funnels of mud when rain fell. The people of Florence braced for the worst, but they did not expect what happened next.

At Penna Hydroelectric Dam, 29 miles from Florence, the massive rainfall raised the water level dangerously high. The operators of the dam realized they had to take some pressure off the dam or it could fail. They were forced to make a decision that made the situation much worse for Florence.

A large mass of water was released from the dam. It flowed swiftly downstream to fill Levan Hydroelectric Dam, 4 miles away. The operators at the Levan Dam didn't think they could hold the additional water, either, so they released it to protect the dam. An enormous wall of water began making a deadly descent toward Florence.

It was the middle of the night as the water approached. Most people in the city were sleeping. They had no idea what was coming. A few who awoke ran to safety before the water came, but most were unaware.

A bridge at the edge of the city

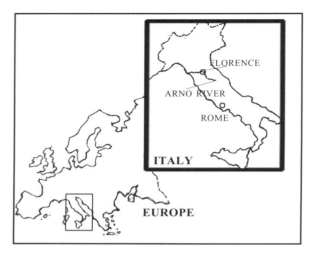

begin shaking violently at 3 A.M. as the water struck it. The entire sewer system of Florence was now backing up, and a terrible stench filled the city.

Slimy rivers of mud were washing down from the hills and mountains. The people of Florence awoke to the sounds of explosions. The floodwaters had struck fuel storage tanks, tearing them open and spewing millions of gallons of oil across the landscape.

At 6 A.M., the floodwaters were a brown torrent filled with wood, rags, and sewage, roaring into Florence. As the dangerous, foul mess reached the doors of the Church of Ognissanti, the priests tried desperately to bar the doors. The water crashed through anyway and flooded the church.

At 7:26 A.M., all power went off. Fifteen feet of water rushed into the Church of Santa Croce. Beautiful paintings, many of them old masterpieces, were ripped from the walls by the rampaging water. At the Florence racetrack, many horses drowned in their stalls before rescuers could reach them.

Nearly 100,000 people rushed to the upper floors or the roofs of their homes to escape the rising water. They huddled there for hours as the rain pelted them. They watched the floodwaters rise, afraid they would not survive. It was not safe to come down until November 4.

As the floodwaters moved back,

the people of Florence faced months of homelessness. Many art treasures and valuable books were destroyed. But only thirty-five people died in Florence in the flood, though more than a hundred died in the heavy rains that struck other cities in Italy at the same time.

About one-third of all deaths from natural disasters are caused by floods. The force of rushing water can destroy vast areas, taking down buildings. But people are learning how to better predict the storms that bring surges of water and how to build stronger dams to control the awesome power of great rivers.

Bibliography

CNN. "Hurricane Andrew Hits U.S. 10 years ago," 8-24-2002.

Frank Leslie's Illustrated Newspaper. "The Conemaugh Calamity," June 15, 1889.

"Hurricane." *The Columbia Encyclopedia*, 7th ed. 1-1-2002.

John Knox National Forum. "Isaac's Storm: A Man, Time, and the Deadliest Hurricane in History," 1-1-2001.

Morgan, Curtis. Knight Ridder/ Tribune News Service. "National Weather Service raises death toll of 1928 Florida Hurricane," 5-9-2003.

National Park Service. "A Roar Like

Thunder," 6-4-2003.

NPR. "Profile: Story of Galveston Hurricane of 1900," 9-8-2000.

NPR. "Robert Marchioli describes his experience living through Hurricane Andrew," 8-23-2002.

New York Times, The. "Johnstown Flood," May 31, 1889.

People Weekly. "Elsie Frum remembers a train's desperate whistle 100 years ago––and the great Johnstown Flood," June 5, 1989, p. 85.

Time. "Out of the Past: Bad Judgment Day," 11-1-99.

Weatherwise. "The Great Galveston Hurricane," 1-11-98.

Whipple, A.B.C., and the editors of Time-Life Books. *Planet Earth: Storm.* Alexandria, Va.: Time-Life Books, 1982.